P9-AQA-934

CeleBRATe!
in
SOUTHeAST
ASIA

BY JOE VIESTI AND DIANE HALL

PHOTOGRAPHED BY JOE VIESTI

LOTHROP, LEE & SHEPARD BOOKS

NEW YORK

(ABOVE) **During Tet Nguyen Dan (Vietnamese New Year) the flower markets of Saigon (officially Ho Chi Minh City) are filled with people buying sprigs of plum blossoms and armloads of flowers to decorate their homes for the celebration.**

(PREVIOUS PAGE) **This Thai girl is all dressed up to attend the Surin Elephant Round-up.**

Text copyright © 1996 by Joe Viesti and Diane Hall

Photographs copyright © 1996 by Joe Viesti

All rights reserved. No part of this book may be reproduced or utilized in any form or by any means, electronic or mechanical, including photocopying and recording, or by any information storage and retrieval system, without permission in writing from the Publisher.

Inquiries should be addressed to Lothrop, Lee & Shepard Books, a division of William Morrow & Company, Inc.,

1350 Avenue of the Americas, New York, New York 10019.

Printed in the United States of America

First Edition   1 2 3 4 5 6 7 8 9 10

Library of Congress Cataloging in Publication Data

Viesti, Joe F. *Celebrate in Southeast Asia* / by Joe Viesti and Diane Hall

p.   cm.   Summary: Describes a variety of holiday celebrations in Southeast Asia,

including Thailand's Elephant Round-Up, Singapore's Moon Cake

Festival, and the Vietnamese New Year.

ISBN 0-688-13488-2. — ISBN 0-688-13489-0 (lib. bdg.)

1. Festivals—Asia, Southeastern—Juvenile literature.

2. Asia, Southeastern—Religious life and customs—Juvenile literature.

[1. Festivals—Asia, Southeastern. 2. Holidays—Asia, Southeastern. 3. Asia, Southeastern—Social life and customs.]

I. Hall, Diane. II. Title. GT4876.5.V54 1996 394.2'6959—dc20 96-6314 CIP AC

Just as we do in the United States, people in Southeast Asia come together to celebrate holidays with song and dance, food and fun, parades and prayer. But the holidays and the ways in which they are celebrated often seem very different from our own. There are many reasons to celebrate—the beginning of the new year, the gathering of the harvest, to commemorate an important event, and to thank God—but whatever and wherever the celebration, it is always a time to forget about workday routines and appreciate the really important things in life: families, beliefs, and traditions. What better way to meet the people of the world than at a celebration!

A Khmer dancer takes the part of a fierce demon during the Chaul Chhnaim (Khmer New Year) celebration in Phnom Penh, Cambodia.

THAILAND

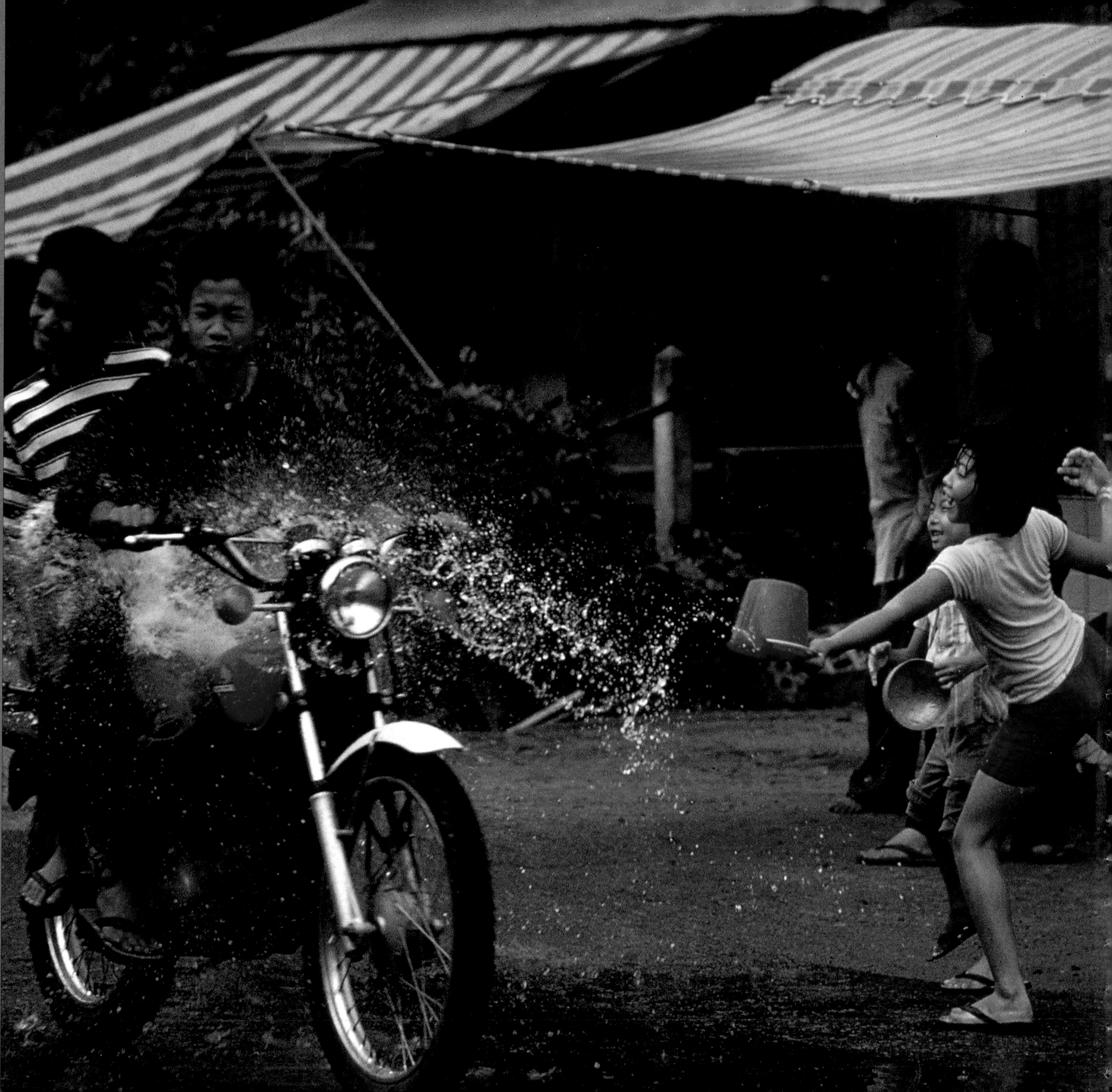

SONGKRAN
(THAI NEW YEAR/WATER FESTIVAL)

These pretty girls are contestants to become the queen of the Chiang Mai water festival.

In Thailand, the new year, called Songkran, is celebrated in April. All over the country, people honor their elders and clean their houses. In some villages they set caged birds free to bring good luck. April is hot and dry in Thailand, so Songkran is first and foremost a water festival.

The festival is normally celebrated for three days, but in Chiang Mai, Thailand's second-largest city, it goes on for a whole week.

A queen of the water festival is chosen to reign over the festivities. Parades of dancers, bands, images of Buddha, sword dancers, and floats welcome the new year. The rivers are filled with people scooping up water with fans and buckets and throwing it at one another. All day long, children throw water on anyone they meet, and everyone gets soaked. But since it's the hottest season of the year, no one complains.

An old Thai myth tells of magical serpents called *nagas* who bring rain by spouting water from the sea. The more they spout, the more rain there will be. During Songkran, children take the place of *nagas*.

SURIN ELEPHANT ROUND-UP

The Suay people of Surin in eastern Thailand have captured and trained wild elephants for centuries, and once each year the trainers, called mahouts, show off their skills. On the third weekend in November, thousands of people come to enjoy the Surin Elephant Round-up. Elephants compete in games of soccer, dance to rock music, and lift huge logs. There's even a game of tug-of-war, with a single elephant at one end of the rope and two hundred Thai soldiers at the other. The celebration ends with a dazzling parade of elephants and mahouts dressed in historic battle costume. As an extra treat, the elephants are available for rides at the end of each day.

(ABOVE) Suay mahouts demonstrate how wild elephants are captured and taught. It can take two to three months to catch the elephants and another six months for training.
(RIGHT) The elephant races are a spectacular sight. Elephants can run surprisingly fast.

THAILAND

Elephants were once a vital part of the Thai army. For hundreds of years the people of Surin captured and trained war elephants for their king. To honor their history, elephants and people wear battle dress copied exactly from an ancient book on war strategy in the climactic procession of the Elephant Round-up.

MALAYSIA

THAIPUSAM
(HINDU DAY OF ATONEMENT)

Thaipusam, the Hindu day of atonement, occurs every year in January or February. The festival celebrates the birthday of Subramanian, the youngest son of the god Shiva. Devout Hindus gather at temples to pray for forgiveness and make offerings of coconuts, milk, honey, and fruits to Subramanian. Thaipusam is also a time to give to the poor.

At the Batu Caves outside the Malaysian capital of Kuala Lumpur, the grounds are trimmed with lights. After sunset on Thaipusam, penitents carry *kavadis*—huge, richly decorated canopies of wood and steel—up the 272 steep steps to the sacred cave. To carry a *kavadi* is a great honor and an act of faith, so the heavier the *kavadi,* the better. Many of the bearers pierce their bodies with skewers to further prove their faith. Onlookers place gifts and offerings in the *kavadis* as they pass.

When the bearers have reached the shrine within the cave, prayers are offered and the skewers are removed. Then the penitents march proudly back down the steps, seemingly unharmed by their grueling ordeal.

(ABOVE) **A** *kavadi* **carrier begins the long climb up to the Batu Caves.**
(LEFT) **Children as well as adults skewer themselves at Thaipusam. Surprisingly, no one seems to bleed or be in pain.**

(ABOVE) Dragon dancers entertain the crowds gathered for the Feast of Lanterns. (RIGHT) The smell of burning sandalwood fills the air as musical bands and dancers swinging lanterns parade under the glow of the full moon.

MOON CAKE FESTIVAL
(MID-AUTUMN FESTIVAL)

The Moon Cake Festival is held to celebrate the overthrow of the Mongol Dynasty in China. According to legend, Chinese rebels hid secret messages inside moon cakes, which are made of a thin rice-flour crust filled with fruit or sweet red bean paste.

The celebration is held in the month of September or October on the night of the full moon. For the Chinese, the full moon is a symbol of unity, and the festival is a time for family togetherness. After a holiday dinner, everyone goes outside to enjoy the full moon, light candles and lanterns, eat moon cakes, and celebrate through the night.

On Moon Cake Night in Singapore, people hold the Feast of Lanterns—a magnificent procession of brilliantly colored lanterns. Dancers and musicians lead the parade through the streets, and a dancing dragon held high on bamboo poles brings up the rear.

SINGAPORE

INDONESIA

KESADA OFFERING

he Kesada Offering takes place in the Tengger Highlands of eastern Java. This mountainous region is holy to the Tenggerese people. It is so isolated that most Javanese call it "the land on the far side of the East."

Each November, on the night of the full moon, the Tenggerese trek to the rim of the Bromo volcano to bring offerings to Brahma, the Hindu god of creation for whom the volcano was named. This custom began over six hundred years ago, when King Hayam Wuruk declared that no one who worshipped Brahma had to pay taxes. Ever since, people have climbed the narrow rim of this eight-thousand-foot active volcano in the middle of the night to throw offerings into the smoking crater. Centuries ago, human beings were sacrificed, but today the offerings consist of coins, vegetables, live chickens, and flowers. If you are brave or foolish enough to climb into the steaming crater, you may keep whatever offerings you can gather.

People climb up winding mountain trails on foot and horseback, guided only by the light of the full moon, to make the Kesada Offering. The sight of dawn on Mount Bromo is well worth the trip.

Bromo is an active volcano. Despite the danger, many people scramble down the steep slopes of the crater to retrieve offerings of coins and food.

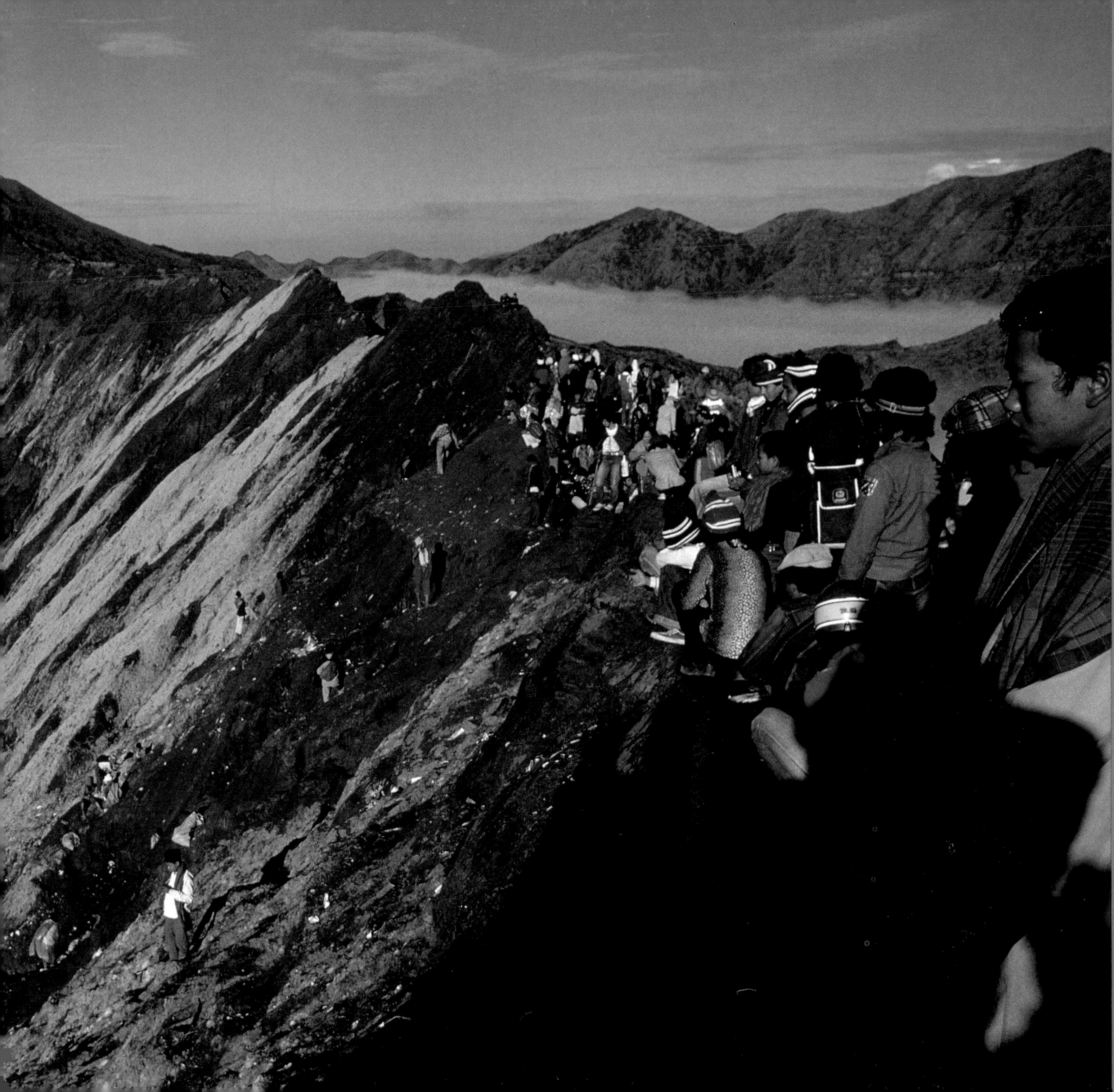

INDONESIA

INDONESIA

CREMATION CEREMONY

In Bali, Indonesia, funerals are not solemn occasions. They are chaotic, noisy, joyful celebrations of the dead person's passage from this world to the next. Cremation, the Balinese believe, frees the spirit from human ties and eases its passage to the home of the gods on Mount Agung, the holiest of Balinese mountains.

After the funeral, the body is placed in a colorful hollow statue.

The Balinese practice a unique blend of Eastern religions, primarily Hindu. They believe burning offerings of money, clothes, and food at a funeral will insure that the deceased wants for nothing in the afterlife.

More than a dozen men lift it to their shoulders, and whirling, zigzagging, and dancing, carry it to the cremation site. The Balinese believe they must keep the spirit from finding its way back to its earthly home or it will be trapped there as a ghost. Everyone in the funeral party shouts to frighten off demons that might attack the spirit along the way. Once the body has been cremated, the spirit is safe with the gods.

Villagers watch as a funeral procession dances its way to the cremation site.

ATI-ATIHAN

Each year during the third week of January, the quiet coastal village of Kalibo in the Philippine Islands awakens to the sound of beating drums. This is the beginning of Ati-Atihan, a riotous three-day festival that celebrates the sale of Panay Island to ten Bornean chieftains in the thirteenth century. The festival also pays tribute to Kalibo's patron saint, Santo Niño (the baby Jesus).

Ati-Atihan is so exuberant that it has been nicknamed the Mardi Gras of the Philippines. People wear wildly colorful costumes and cover their bodies with soot to resemble the original Kalibo natives, the Atis. Then they dance and sing through the streets just as the Atis did when the Borneans purchased Panay Island from them more than seven hundred years ago. The dancing continues late into the night, as everyone chants *hala Bira!*—Keep going!—and *puera pasma!*—No tiring!

"Tribes" of identically dressed dancers march through the streets of Kalibo, singing songs that have been passed down for hundreds of years.

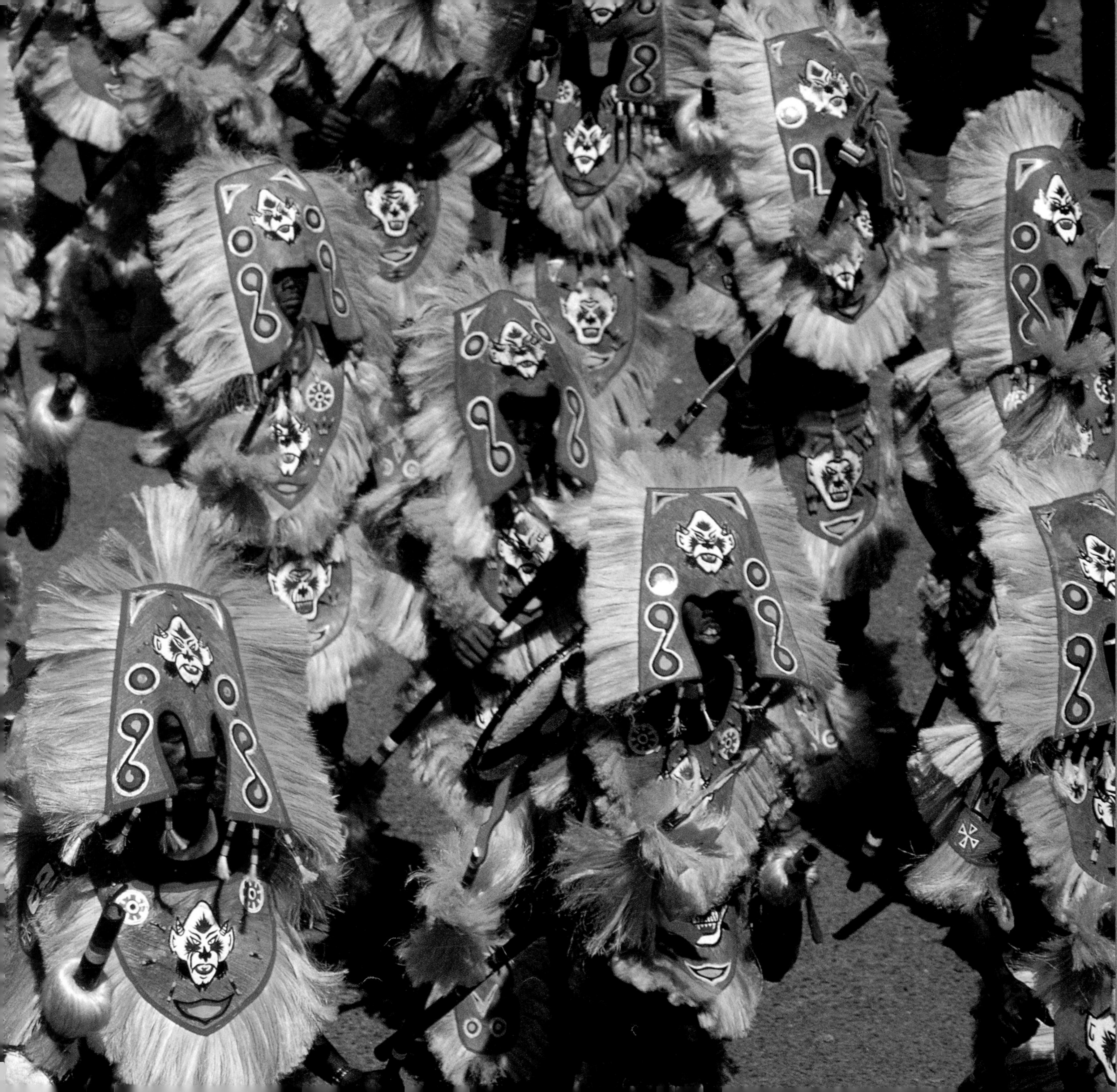

PHILIPPINES

APALIT RIVER FESTIVAL
(FEAST OF SAINT PETER AND SAINT PAUL)

The Catholic feast day of Saint Peter and Saint Paul falls in late June. It's not surprising that the fisherfolk of Apalit, Philippines, chose Saint Peter, a fisherman, as their patron saint. They call him *Apong Iro*, which means Grandfather Iro.

The Apalit River Festival lasts for three days, and the major event is the four-mile river parade. Life-sized statues of the saints are carried through the streets to the riverfront while brass bands play and the villagers dance through town. At the banks of the river, the saints are placed in pagodas mounted on barges. The magnificent pagodas have several tiers, all decorated with brightly colored paper flowers and gold leaf. A flotilla of decorated boats joins the barges, and the parade sails past the village to the sounds of music and cheering merrymakers, both on shore and off, who seem to never stop dancing.

Everyone in Apalit wants to be part of the floating parade called a *caracol*. Every boat on the river is overflowing with happy people.

TET
(VIETNAMESE NEW YEAR)

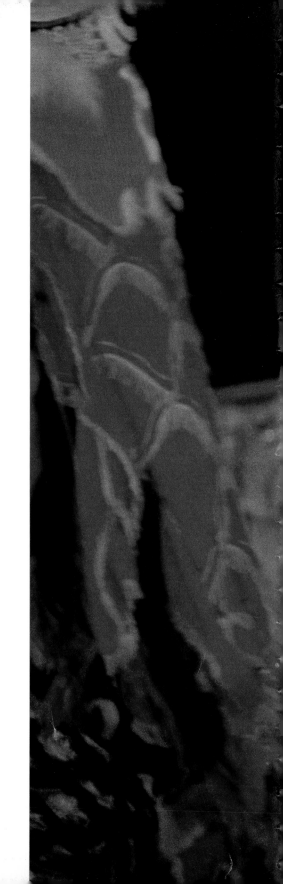

Tet Nguyen Dan, Tet for short, is the most important festival of the year for the Vietnamese. This new year's celebration falls in January or early February and lasts for seven days, during which people hold family reunions, pay their debts, and settle arguments. It's also known as the "firecracker festival." At midnight on the first day, the festival begins with a BANG, and the sound of firecrackers going off fills the air for the rest of the holiday.

Before Tet begins, women spend days making *banh chung* (sticky rice cakes wrapped in banana leaves and tied with bamboo) to give to friends and relatives as new year's gifts. *Banh chung* symbolize the Vietnamese people's gratitude for the earth's abundance.

The Vietnamese believe that the first week of the new year will set the pattern for the rest of the year. Homes are cleaned to sparkling, and everyone buys new clothes to start the year off right. In Saigon (officially Ho Chi Minh City), families go to huge flower markets to buy flowers and new year's trees. All over the city, the streets are filled with people—on bikes, motorcycles, and every other vehicle imaginable—carrying their trees home to ward off evil spirits.

Tet is a wonderful time to visit Vietnam, for visitors are considered very important then, especially the first visitor of the new year.

Dragon dancing is a traditional part of the Tet celebration. As the dragons leap and romp through the crowded streets, strings of firecrackers dangling from poles several stories high fill the sky with mock thunder and lightning.

THAT LUANG FESTIVAL

Every year in November, thousands of Buddhists come to the Pha That Luang, located on the outskirts of Vientiane, Laos, for the week-long That Luang Festival. Built in 1566, the Pha That Luang is the most important monument in Laos. This golden stupa, a towerlike Buddhist shrine, sits atop a pyramid surrounded by thirty smaller spires, symbolizing the thirty levels of perfection in the Buddhist faith.

The first level of perfection, charity to the poor, is practiced on a grand scale during the That Luang Festival. Each day, hundreds of Buddhist monks and nuns, who have taken a vow of poverty, gather at the Pha That Luang to receive alms. Thousands of people stream past them, passing out gifts of food (especially sticky rice), candy, money, and flowers.

A fair is held on the temple grounds during festival week, where a variety of traditional Laotian foods are sold for picnics and offerings. There are also amusements, rides, and exhibits of Laotian handicrafts and products.

The festival comes to a close on the night of the full moon. Strings of lights illuminate the Pha That Luang, and throngs of people gather for a candlelight procession followed by a dazzling fireworks display.

(LEFT) There are thirty steps to perfection in the Buddhist faith. This boy is taking the first step: charity. (RIGHT) Buddhist nuns sit patiently at the base of the Pha That Luang, waiting for another wave of eager alms givers.

(ABOVE) Top: Vendors prepare picnic food on the temple grounds for hungry celebrants. Center: Young as they are, these boys are already monks. Bottom: Flowers, cash, and sticky rice fill one alms bowl. (RIGHT) Fireworks burst over the lighted spire of the Pha That Luang. Not only does this ancient stupa house a relic believed to be Buddha's breastbone, it is also a symbol of Laotian independence.

LAOS

CHAUL CHHNAIM
(KHMER NEW YEAR)

Chaul Chhnaim, the Cambodian (or Khmer) New Year, is celebrated for three days beginning on April 13. The Khmer people believe that beginning the new year with a messy house invites bad luck, so houses are cleaned and decorated inside and out. People also visit temples, where they offer prayers and sprinkle the Buddhas with water for good luck in the coming year. Many leave behind small mounds of sand in the temple yard as a prayer for a life with as many days as there are grains of sand.

King Sihanouk takes part in a Chaul Chhnaim ceremony at Wat Phnom.

In Phnom Penh, Cambodia's capital city, the Wat Phnom is *the* place to observe the New Year. This temple sits atop a tree-covered hill that can be seen from anywhere in the city. A grand staircase, with lion statues and railings in the form of mythical snakes called *nagas*, leads to the temple's main entrance. This is where the king of Cambodia celebrates the new year. Dancers in traditional costumes surround the entrance as he climbs the staircase, led by a procession of Buddhist monks. Crowds of people gather to celebrate with him, everyone hoping to be among the lucky few who receive a traditional new year's gift of batik cloth from the hands of the king.

Buddhist monks lead the New Year's procession up the grand staircase to the entrance of Wat Phnom.